GW00771342

I have
ASTHMA

I have ASTHMA

Brenda Pettenuzzo

meets

Alex Wood

Photography: Chris Fairclough

Consultants: The Asthma Society

FRANKLIN WATTS

London/New York/Sydney/Toronto

Alexander James Wood is nine years old. He suffers from asthma. He has two sisters, Sarah, aged thirteen, who also has asthma, and Louise, eleven. Their father, Stephen, works for a large bank, and their mother, Ann, is a secretary. The family live in Essex.

Contents

©1988 Franklin Watts
12a Golden Square
LONDON W1

ISBN: 0 86313 745 8

Series Consultant: Beverley Mathias
Editor: Jenny Wood
Design: Edward Kinsey

Typesetting: Keyspools Ltd

Printed in Hong Kong

The Publishers, Photographer and author would like to thank Alex Wood and his family for their great help and co-operation in the preparation of this book.

Thanks are also due to Staples Road County Primary School, The Hospital for Sick Children, Great Ormond Street and The Asthma Society for their help and advice.

Brenda Pettenuzzo is a Science and Religious Education teacher at St Angela's Ursuline Convent School, a Comprehensive School in the London Borough of Newham.

Life before asthma

"When I was a baby, no one in our family had asthma. My big sister was the first person to get it."

Alex and his two older sisters were all very healthy babies who didn't seem to get coughs and colds very often. Neither of their parents and none of their grandparents had ever had asthma or any similar conditions. When Alex was about three years old, his sister Sarah, then seven, developed asthma. She was referred to the Hospital for Sick Children, Great Ormond Street, London and has been treated by them ever since.

The first attack

"I was six when I first got asthma. It started when I had a cold."

Alex's first asthma attack was quite severe. He found it very difficult to breathe. Fortunately his parents recognised the symptoms and took him to hospital straightaway. On that first visit Alex stayed in hospital for three days. He soon had another spell in hospital, and when he left he had several different medicines to take every day.

Check-ups

"I have a check-up at Great Ormond Street every six months. If I get ill I might go sooner, or I might go to a hospital near my home."

The specialist at Great Ormond Street has made an arrangement with the hospital where Alex was first admitted. It is nearer to his home. If he becomes very ill, his parents or their doctor can arrange for him to be taken there at once. They telephone the hospital and everything he needs is ready when they arrive.

"The first thing that happens when I go for my check-up is that I'm weighed and measured."

The nurses at the clinic weigh and measure all their patients. They write the information on to each patient's record card. Steady weight gain and growth are signs of healthy normal development. If Alex's asthma were really severe it might slow down his growth.

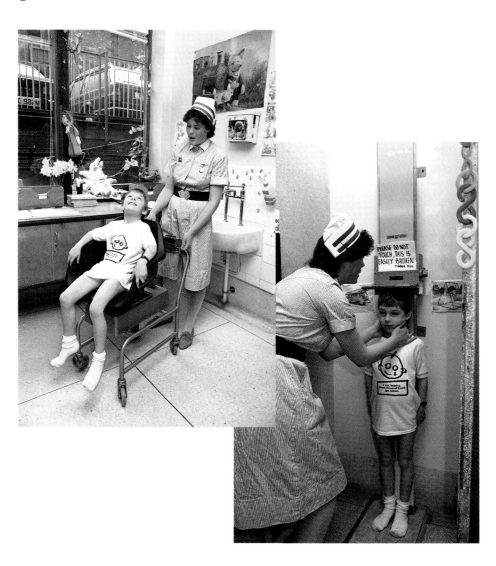

"The doctor listens to my chest then looks at my ears, nose and throat."

Alex has a medical check-up to make sure that his throat and lungs are all right. The doctor also talks to him about how he has been feeling lately. Asthma can make children quite frightened, so it is important to talk to them about it. Alex keeps a diary. In it he and his mum keep a record of what medicines he has taken, and how he has been feeling. The doctor looks at this diary as well.

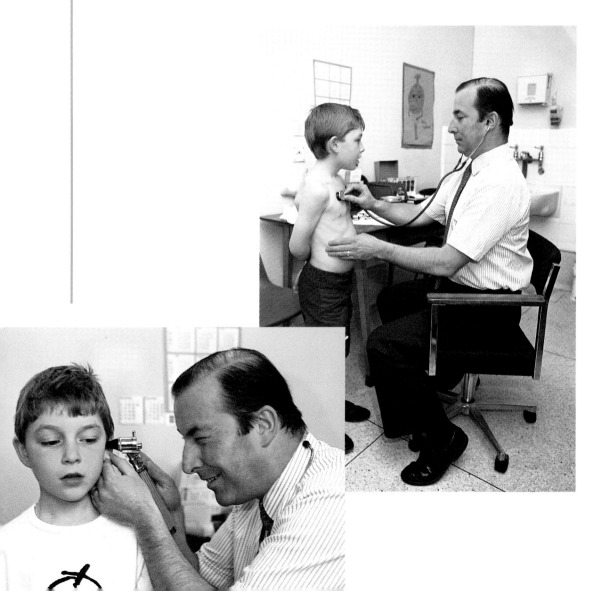

"The doctor measures my 'peak flow'. Sometimes I go to the respiratory unit as well. There I have to run around for five minutes and then measure my lungs with another machine."

The "peak flow" measurement is an indicator of how well the lungs are working. During an asthma attack the tubes through which air travels get narrow. It becomes more difficult to blow out. The meter shows how hard Alex is blowing. Sometimes the "peak flow" level drops before an asthma attack starts. This means it is a useful early warning sign.

"I've had allergy tests done at the hospital. They put lots of things on my skin to see which ones would make it swell up."

Many people who have asthma find that it comes on when they are in contact with certain foods or animals or other things. This is called "allergic asthma". Other people suffer asthma attacks when they do strenuous exercise. Alex seems to get asthma when he is suffering from mild infections such as colds and sore throats. At the hospital the doctors have found that he is allergic to a few things, but none of these seems to provoke his asthma too badly. His parents try to keep him away from the things he is allergic to anyway.

On holiday

"We sometimes go to foreign countries for our holidays. We have to make sure that we have taken all my medicines with us, and Sarah's as well!"

Since Sarah and Alex developed asthma the family have taken the same sort of holidays as before. They have travelled to many countries by plane and by car and boat. The hospital loans them a portable nebuliser for these trips. (A nebuliser helps patients to inhale certain medicines.) Alex's parents always find out about local hospitals and doctors before they set off. So far, there has never been a serious emergency while they have been abroad.

At school

"At school the teachers know about my asthma. It doesn't cause any problems for me or for them."

Alex does everything that the other children in his class do. Sometimes he feels himself getting breathless and asks to sit down quietly for a while. On a few occasions his mum has had to come and take him home or to the doctor. Like most children who have asthma, Alex has missed very little school through his illness.

"I eat a packed lunch at school. I like it better than school dinner."

Alex's family are careful about what they eat. They try to eat a balanced, healthy diet. Many people who have asthma have to avoid certain foods. Sometimes children are allergic to quite common things, such as milk or eggs. Others have to avoid nuts or beans. There is a wide range of foods and other substances which can cause asthma or other reactions. Alex doesn't seem to be affected in this way by the things he eats, but his mum is careful about his packed lunch anyway.

"After lunch I use my inhaler. I need this one three times a day, but I have another one that I use twice."

It is important to use regularly the medicines the doctors have prescribed. Children who have asthma have to remember to use their inhalers at the right time. Younger children might have to be reminded by their teacher. Alex is old enough to remember by himself. He keeps his inhaler in his packed lunch box so he will remember to use it after he has finished eating.

Sports and hobbies

"My dad and I go swimming every week at our local pool. Sometimes we let my sisters come too, but usually it's just dad and me."

Some people suffer from "exercise asthma". Their attacks come on after taking strenuous exercise. This sort of asthma is always worse when the air is cold or dry. Swimming is good exercise for people with asthma. The air at the pool is usually warm and damp. It doesn't cause irritation to the lung tubes. Some asthma sufferers have become world-class swimmers.

"I am a Cub Scout and my sisters are both Guides. Our meetings are on different days but we always go to church parade together."

Many years ago children with asthma were thought of as "delicate". They were not allowed out very much and their parents looked after them carefully. Fortunately this is not the attitude of Alex's parents. They want him and his sisters to enjoy life and be as active as possible. Alex and his sisters take part in many activities, and have found great enjoyment through the Scouts and Guides.

"I like all sport but at the moment cricket is my favourite. I'm in the 'Futurestars' coaching programme."

Alex is taking part in a cricket programme for boys of his age. He plays indoors every week at a school near his home. The scheme is organised by the local District Council and the Sports Council. When he is older and if he gets good enough, he may join a local Cricket Club. Like swimming, cricket is a good sport for people with asthma, especially if they have exercise asthma.

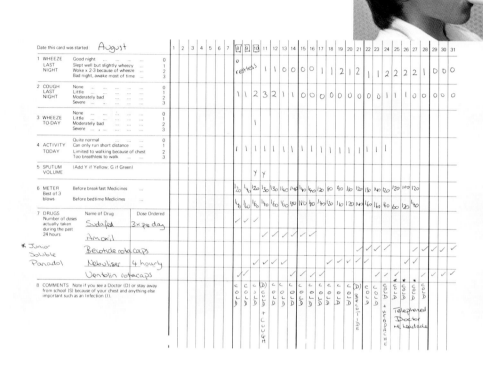

Living with asthma

"I have to measure my 'peak flow' every night and every morning. We write it down in my diary."

Alex uses a simple version of the hospital "peak flow" machine at home. He blows into it and a marker shows how hard he has puffed. When his "peak flow" is lower than normal for his age and size it usually means he is having a bout of asthma. Sometimes the "peak flow" rate drops before the asthma starts. If the "peak flow" is very low, his parents know that he should go to hospital. They can arrange this through their family doctor. In a serious emergency they can telephone the hospital themselves.

"My sister and I have lots of different inhalers. Every now and again our doctor changes which one we use."

Several different types of medicines are used to treat asthma. Each type can be given in various ways. Some people use capsules which contain powder. The capsules are broken and the powder is inhaled. Some people use an inhaler which "puffs" the medicine into their lungs as they breathe in. Some inhalers adapt one of these methods to make it easier for younger children to use. Alex is using a Nebuhaler, and Sarah is using a Spacer.

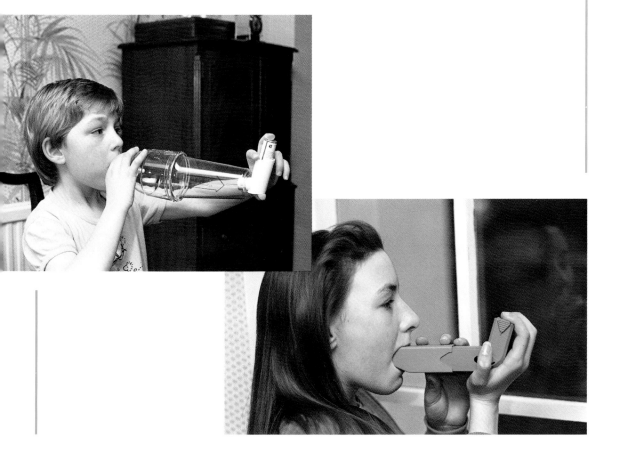

"Sometimes if I am very wheezy, my inhalers don't work fast enough to stop me getting worse. Then I have to use my nebuliser."

The nebuliser blows air through the medicine and changes it to a mist. It can then be inhaled through a face mask or a mouthpiece. This gets the medicine into the lungs much faster than any other method. Alex has a nebuliser at home. Some people with asthma have to use one every day, sometimes in the middle of the night as well. Alex only needs to use his if he is particularly ill, but not serious enough to have to go to hospital.

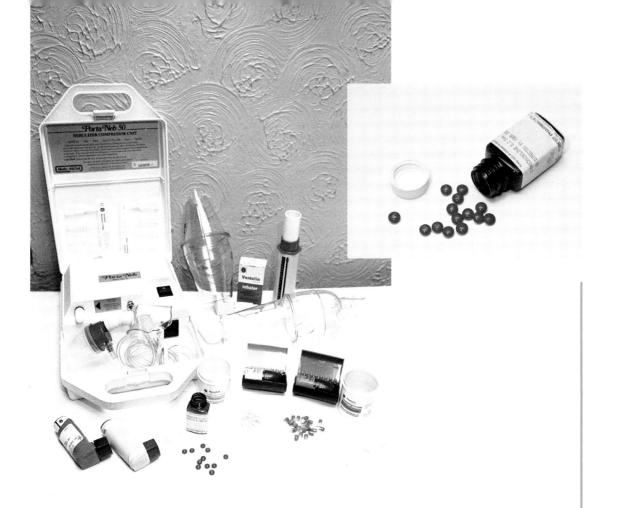

"I have lots of different medicines at home, but I don't use them all at once."

Compared to some asthmatic children, Alex takes quite a lot of drugs. The family doctor and the hospital specialist tell Alex's parents which medicines to use. They keep a course of steroid tablets at home to use in emergencies. These tablets have to be taken in a special way. Alex starts with four a day, then gradually cuts down to one before stopping altogether. Usually the steroids will stop Alex's attack from getting bad enough for him to need admitting to hospital.

Favourite pets

"I like all animals, especially wild ones. I have two reptiles, and my favourite is the lizard."

Many people who have asthma are allergic to furry or feathered animals. Pets can be a problem, even when they belong to someone else. Alex's sister has a rabbit, but it lives outside the house and doesn't cause him any problem. For some reason, people do not develop allergies to animals such as fish and reptiles. Alex has found that the lizard and his slow worm are the perfect pets.

With the family

"I play table football with my sisters in the garden. We can't play in the house because we make so much noise!"

Being the youngest in the family means that Alex doesn't get any special treatment. Although he knows that asthma can be quite serious, his two big sisters help him to be sensible about it. Everyone knows what to do if Alex has a severe attack. While he is well, he and everyone else behave as if there is nothing wrong with him.

"We do lots of things together in my family. We have lots of games which we play at home."

Alex's parents try to treat him as normally as possible, but they know how serious asthma can be. It can be very worrying to be the parents of asthmatic children. The whole family, including grandparents, has tried to learn as much as possible about asthma. Thanks to this sensible attitude, Alex and his sister Sarah have been able to lead full and normal lives.

Facts about asthma

Over two million people suffer from asthma in the UK. About half start suffering as children, but many of these grow out of their asthma in their teens. Asthma is very common in children, and it is estimated that one in ten children suffers from asthma.

You cannot "catch" asthma from another person, in the way that you might "catch" chickenpox or measles. Some people inherit a tendency to asthma, but this does not mean that they will become asthmatic. Asthma will only develop if it is triggered at some stage in life. In many cases, modern methods of treatment control asthma very easily. But some people are more seriously affected, and there are nearly two thousand deaths from asthma each year in the UK.

Asthma affects the breathing tubes in the lungs. Air reaches the lungs through a series of tubes arranged something like the branches of a tree, but upside-down. Breath is taken in through the tree trunk, then passes into two main branches, which divide further into smaller and smaller branches. The smallest branches carry air into the lung tissue itself. In a healthy person the tubes, however narrow, are always open to the passage of air.

When asthma occurs, the breathing tubes become narrow, their linings become swollen, and a thick mucus coating is produced. This makes breathing very difficult. There is usually a feeling of tightness deep in the chest, and often an irritating cough. The passage of air through the narrowed tubes can make a whistling noise – the characteristic "wheeze" of the asthma sufferer.

An attack of asthma may come on suddenly and go away again just as quickly, or it may persist for several days. Some older people suffer from almost full-time breathlessness, which varies in intensity. This state is called "chronic asthma".

There are many triggers for asthma. Some people suffer from "allergic asthma". Allergy is an oversensitivity to something which is quite common and causes no problem to most people. An allergic individual may find their eyes become red and itchy when they touch or inhale the substance they are allergic to. They may sneeze, break out in a rash, their face may swell, or they may suffer an asthma attack.

The most common causes of allergic asthma are pollen, house

dust (and the mites which live in the dust), animals (hair and flakes of dead skin in dogs, but saliva in cats), drugs and foods. Many people find that contact with the "allergen" – the substance to which they are allergic – does not always provoke an asthma attack. Their reaction may vary according to the time of day, the time of the year, and their state of health. Some attacks of allergic asthma are brought on by things which are inhaled, and some by things which are ingested, or eaten. When an obvious allergy to a particular thing can be identified, then the asthma can be controlled by avoiding that thing. Unfortunately asthma is rarely caused by an allergy to only one substance, but allergic asthma is one of the easiest to treat with drugs. As well as those which help by keeping the breathing tubes open, there are anti-allergy drugs available which dampen down the body's reactions to allergens.

Some people suffer from asthma which comes on after exercise. This is called "exercise-induced asthma" or simply "exercise asthma". With this form of asthma the "wheeze" and cough come after the exercise has stopped. It is not like the normal breathlessness which comes with all strenuous exercise.

Some people suffer from exercise asthma alone, but some suffer from other forms of asthma as well. Some people get exercise asthma only when they have a cold or when there is a lot of pollen about. As with other forms of asthma, the severity of the attacks varies from person to person and according to the time of the day or year. Exercise asthma can be controlled by taking extra doses of prescribed medicines before exercise, and many doctors advise their patients to do this. It is also possible for a person to choose types of exercise which will keep them fit without bringing on an asthma attack. Swimming is particularly useful, especially in indoor pools. Warm, moist air is very soothing for people with asthma. Sports such as cricket, sprinting and jumping, where the exercise is in short bursts rather than long spells, tend not to trigger an attack. This is especially true if the air is not very cold.

Another cause of asthma, especially in children under the age of seven, is virus infection. Some people have no symptoms whatsoever until they catch a common cold or get a chest infection or sore throat. Then a severe asthma attack may come on quite suddenly. For many children this is their first experience of asthma. It can be very distressing to them and to their parents. In many cases this type of asthma requires hospital treatment to get it under control, but once it has been stabilised there is often no more need for concern.

There have been many advances in the treatment of asthma during the last twenty to thirty years. Research is being carried out all over the world into all aspects of asthma and its treatment. At the moment there is no cure for asthma, but the better our understanding of the way in which it occurs, the more likely it is that a cure may one day be found.

The treatments for asthma can be divided into two main types: those which relieve the symptoms, and those which protect sufferers from attacks. The first group includes those drugs which are called "bronchodilators". These are chemicals which cause the air tubes, or bronchi, to dilate (grow wider). They have the effect of opening up the narrowed air passages during an attack. There are different types of bronchodilators: some work by relaxing the muscles in the walls of the air tubes, others work against the nerves which cause the muscles to tighten in the first place. Bronchodilators can be given in various ways: syrups, tablets, inhalers or injections. Doctors choose the most suitable

method for each patient. Many asthmatics have an inhaler which they use regularly, with another type for more serious attacks. Occasionally doctors may need to inject bronchodilators in order to bring a very severe attack under control.

The second group of medicines are those which protect the sufferer from getting an attack in the first place. These can be either anti-inflammatory (that is, they dampen down the inflammation in the swollen air passages) or anti-allergenic.

The anti-inflammatory drugs are mostly steroids. These are known for their side-effects when taken in large and regular doses. Fortunately, when steroids are used to treat asthma, they are usually inhaled and have very little effect on other parts of the body. Sometimes people have to take courses of steroid tablets, or have steroids given by injection or intravenous drip in hospital. Even then, if the drug is taken or given correctly, there is very little chance of any unpleasant side-effects. In many circumstances, steroids have proved life-savers for asthmatics having serious attacks.

The best-known anti-allergenic drug for asthma is Intal. This was discovered several years ago and has been bringing relief to many asthmatics, especially children, ever since.

The Asthma Society & Friends of the Asthma Research Council

The aim of the Society is to help asthmatics to understand and control their condition so that they can live healthier and more active lives. Funds are also raised for medical research undertaken by the parent organisation, the Asthma Research Council.

Membership of the Asthma Society is open to all asthmatics and all persons interested in their welfare.

New members are put in touch with a local branch where possible, unless indicated otherwise on the application form, in which case postal membership is maintained through the central office.

Any member who is willing can assist in branch activities.

Running branch meetings, fund-raising, secretarial work, organising and running swim groups are just some of the ways in which members can help to support a branch.

The Society's newspaper, *Asthma News*, is published three times a year. Also available are leaflets on the treatment, care and understanding of asthma.

The Society sponsors activity holidays for asthmatic children. It provides grants for those unable to afford the cost.

Further information can be obtained from:

Asthma Society & Friends of the Asthma Research Council, 300 Upper Street, Islington, London N1 2XX.

Glossary

Allergen A substance which can bring about an allergic reaction in some individuals.

Allergy An unexpected reaction in some individuals to common everyday substances which cause other people no problems at all. An allergy may show itself in various ways – skin rash or hay fever (irritation of the nose, throat and eyes), for example, as well as asthma.

Bronchodilator A substance which causes the "bronchi" (the tubes which carry air to the lungs) to dilate, or grow wider. This makes breathing easier.

Inflammation A swollen and irritable condition of body tissues which may be caused by allergy, infection or chemicals.

Inhaler A device which can be used to introduce drugs into the body's respiratory (breathing) system.

Intravenous drip A method of putting drugs directly into the bloodstream.

Mucus A thick, slippery liquid that protects the body's membrane, the soft, smooth tissue that lines most of the inner passages of the body.

Nebuliser A device which makes a mist out of a liquid by blowing air or oxygen through it. It can be used to deliver various medicines directly to the lungs.

Peak flow This is a measurement of how fast someone can blow air out of their lungs when they are trying as hard as they can. Taking regular "peak flow" measurements is a useful way of monitoring the state of the breathing tubes.

Physiotherapy The use of massage, exercise and sometimes heat treatment to help people suffering from disease, injury or deformity. It can assist breathing problems. A person trained to do this is called a physiotherapist.

Pollen The substance produced by the male parts of flowering plants. Pollen can be very troublesome for people who are allergic to it.

Steroids A large group of naturally occurring substances which have certain chemical features in common. Many steroids play important roles in the body. Most of the steroids used in treating asthma are made in laboratories and are not naturally occurring.

Index